ALWAYS DO YOUR BEST

GUIDE TO BE A TOP ACHIEVER

MARC SHAMUS

iMasterLife.com

Copyright © 2016 by Marc Shamus

All rights reserved. No part of this publication may be produced, transmitted, transcribed, stored in a retrieval system, or translated into any language, in any form, by any means, without written permission of the author. Understand that the information contained in this book is an opinion, and should be used for personal entertainment purposes only. You are responsible for your own behavior, and this book is not to be considered medical, legal, or personal advice. Nor is this book to be understood as putting forth any cure for any type of acute or chronic psychological illness. The programs and information expressed within this book are not medical or psychological advice, but rather represent the author's opinions and are solely for informational and educational purposes only. The Author and the publisher do not hold any responsibility for errors, omissions or contrary interpretation of the subject matter herein.

Edited by:

Marc Shamus

Published by:

i Master Life Publishing

Always Do Your Best / Marc Shamus
ISBN-13: 978-1-945719-03-5

CONTENTS

Personal Message from Marc Shamus I

Introduction 1

Download Your Goal Setting Guide 4

Note from the Publisher 5

SECTION I
ENVIRONMENT 7

   1. Never Be Afraid to Ask for Help 8

   2. Surround Yourself with Other Achievers 9

   3. Compare Yourself to No One 10

SECTION II
TIME 11

   1. Preparation is the Foundation 12

   2. Budget Your Time Wisely 13

   3. Take a Break to Regain Clarity 14

SECTION III
ETHICS 15
1. Work Hard to Get Results 16
2. Continually Strive to Do Better 17
3. Nobody Likes a Cheater 18
4. I Hate Liars 19

SECTION IV
MINDSET 21
1. Belief Breathes Life into Creating Success 22
2. Adjust Your Attitude to Propel Your Results 24
3. Tomorrow is Another Day 25
4. Reward Yourself for Victories 26
5. You Don't Have to Be First 28

SECTION V
PERFORMANCE 31
1. Keep Your Eyes on Your Target Goals 32
2. Laziness Gets You Nowhere 33
3. Halfway is No Way 34
4. Quitting is Not an Option 35
5. Excuses are for Losers 36

Closing	37
About the Author	38
Personal Dedication	39
Did You Love Always Do Your Best?	40
More Recommended Publications	41
Watch Our Video Courses	42

Personal Message from Marc Shamus

I wrote this book because of the very rigid upbringing I received. My parents held extremely high ideals in our household. There was a firm mindset that there was exclusively one single choice in life; high performance. No other option was available and to speak of it, or to think of it was not even given due feasibility.

Mom and Dad had colossal hopes for my future and craved to establish the uttermost sufficient environment around me to satisfy this becoming a reality. On all occasions, they would speak their words of wisdom to immerse me in a consciousness of creation. Seeing things from lack or feeling deficiencies was just not a part of the appropriate logic to pursue a happy life.

From a very young age, Mom and Dad encouraged me to go all out and pursue personal abundance. They instilled in me the thirst to improve myself and never settle for less than outstanding. Growing up, I saw them get sorrowful, irritable and discontented when I did not apply myself to my complete capabilities. There was no question what their aim was. They sought to generate inside of me the ambition to win at whatever I spent time concentrating on.

I want to reciprocate in advance the awareness I have from being raised this fashion to other folks. There are enormous insights I can contribute stemming from my background. In the writing of **ALWAYS DO YOUR BEST**, I am able to teach strategies that have given me advantages in my life to rise to the top and attain fascinating consummations.

Why You Should Read This Book

As you read this book, be willing to undergo transformation. Be truthful to yourself of your current progress in life activities and be eager to soak up concepts I explain. They can be the catalyst which can stimulate huge noticeable necessary adjustments in your life.

This book will help you gain the knowledge of the various mentalities at hand that can work to your benefit. It will give you some of the finest solutions to yield life favorable conclusions. It will then be up to you to practice imperative activities to carry out approaches taught in this book, **ALWAYS DO YOUR BEST**. You must put in the work and employ "Do" mode to conceive results.

You can take your life from ordinary to extraordinary with this new gained knowledge. What you do with it is truly up to you. I am rooting you on all the way as you read this book and start on the journey to the new amazing fortunate victorious YOU!!!!

INTRODUCTION

My parents both grew up without acquiring extraordinary treatment from others. Everything they accomplished came from their own sweat equity. They had to put in the efforts and materialize the future they wanted.

Each had their own separate experiences before they came together as a couple. The magic is how their philosophy of Always Do Your Best was a compatibility they both shared and thus they built a strong future together from applying it to rearing a family.

My mother, Phyllis Shamus, was a quiet, polite and fair woman in her young years. Her father, Harold Mickelson, was the only parent who worked and he did well for being a blue collar worker, yet money was tight.

Harold (my grandfather) believed strongly in always putting your best foot forward. I used to hear him say this from time to time. That same energy rolled over into my mom and she would remind me about this philosophy at all turns.

My father, Richard Shamus, was an eager, ambitious, honest and loyal man in his young years. Both his mom, Margaret Shamus and his father, Jesse Shamus worked and each excelled at their chosen fields.

They made very decent income and collectively held the ideology that hard work gets you where you want to go in life. That same spirit transferred to my dad and he would emphasize this to me every chance he had.

December 1974 with my family; Left to Right: Phyllis Shamus, I (Marc Shamus), Arnold Shamus and Richard Shamus

Throughout my young years, I feel quit fortunate to have been exposed to such reasoning. It all began under the roof of my mom and dad's house that I flourished and learned the skills to be all that I wanted to be in life.

As my life progressed, I rose to the pinnacle of many distinctive arenas, while utilizing the same success orientated doctrine each time.

I channeled my attention on enacting the life lessons that I learned that would enable me to <u>always do my best</u>!

July 1997 spending quality time with Mom and Dad

I will cover in this book the 20 main life lessons that my mom and dad taught me so I could always do my best. Each lesson is important for you to master and be able to propel your own life into warp drive towards massive success. Remember, it is crucial, that you always do your best too!

Without further ado, here we go.

DOWNLOAD YOUR GOAL SETTING GUIDE

Get access to your FREE goal setting guide by going to

http://iMasterLife.com/GoalBonus

Inside the bonus guide, you'll discover...

• What are the Building Blocks of success

• How to set up Success Planning to reach goals

• Very powerful methods of Implementing Success

• 10X your chances of reaching goals via Success Management

NOTE FROM THE PUBLISHER

i Master Life
EMPOWERING . ENGAGING . TRANSFORMING

Thank you for purchasing this **i Master Life Publishing** book. Our goal is to get high quality Life Mastery materials and other worthwhile media into the hands of incredible people like you.

FOLLOW US:

Join our mailing list and get updates on new releases, deals, bonus content and other great publications from **i Master Life Publishing**.

iMasterLife.com/fan

SUPPORT US:

If you enjoyed this or any of our other books, would you please help support **I Master Life**. The sustainable revenue you provide ensures we can continue to provide publishing the very best media possible for you.

Just go to this link:
iMasterLife.com/fund

Thank You!

Marc A. Shamus
Founder

SECTION I
ENVIRONMENT

DEFINITION

1) The aggregate of social and cultural conditions that you live or work in influence the life of an individual or community, especially toward how people feel or how effectively people can work; milieu.

2) The sum total of all surrounding objects of a living organism, including natural forces and other living things, which provide conditions and circumstances for development and growth as well as of danger and damage.

1. Never Be Afraid to Ask for Help

Asking for help is not a sign of weakness. The opposite is actually the truth. It takes a pretty brave soul to admit they do not have all the answers and are needing assistance.

All Go-Getters from time to time get stumped on something and have a choice to make. They can either be too proud to seek help and get stuck in a rut or they can be honest with themselves, lower their ego and find the most suitable person to help them. Never be afraid to ask for help.

One of the top reasons people end up plateauing or quitting things is due to having unanswered questions. People who are in confusion tend to do nothing. The key is to not stay stuck with confusion long and to never stop being in engagement mode.

Both of those are killers of productivity. They will quickly stop you dead in your tracks from receiving quantifiable results. Be conscious of the frustrations you encounter and intuitively know when to ask for help to move forward to your next success.

2. Surround Yourself with Other Achievers

Who we are around is super instrumental in creating the right mental and lingual environment for cultivating victory. It only makes sense that if you surround yourself with other achievers, their ability to perform well will rub off on you since you will spend a considerable amount of time around these people.

On the flip side, if you immerse yourself around people that are not chasing greatness and just settle for whatever results show up, you are going to severely face a disappointing, inferior outcome. Who you are allocating your time to, always directly manifests the raising or lowering of your energetic vibration and your ability to get into peak state.

Top Achievers know that you want to prime your skills and sharpen your abilities. Being around other people who are also constantly being the best versions of themselves, this will push you to elevate your game of life too.

A fire invariably burns hotter when the embers in it are all hot. In the same strain of thought, if you are an ember, your fire can be cooled off by being around those people who possess no heat (no passion to do their best)..

3. COMPARE YOURSELF TO NO ONE

Every single person is special and has varying talents. Even twin siblings are diverse from one another. Be kind and compare yourself to no one. There is no reason for alarm just because one person may be flying sky high and attaining out of this world results and you may be struggling to stamp out even a small result. The battle is not going on outside of you, so if you buy into the philosophy that external factors are making all the difference, you may be missing the point.

The real dilemma is the battle of the mind. The only real struggle in life is you against you. It is the paradox that drives us on and frustrates the heck out of us. If you really want to compare anything, then contrast your efforts and outcomes of now to what you have been able to do in the past.

That is the true measurement which may count and simultaneously inspire you to be better. Just don't fall in the pitfall of negative self-fulfilling prophesy due to lack of past performance on a project. Past performance does not equal future performance. Believe yourself possible to do anything and keep an open mind while pursuing it. You will do just fine.

SECTION II
<u>TIME</u>

DEFINITION

1) The indefinite continued progress of existence and events in the past, present, and future regarded as a whole.

2) Plan, schedule, or arrange when (something) should happen or be done.

1. Preparation is the Foundation

Preparation is the invisible force that binds increased possibilities and secures the longevity of us being able to quest after victories and then sustain them. Preparation is the foundation that all the other effort we provide later on builds upon.

Winners prepare and plan for success. Preparation is the first stage we all go through when we are embarking on an important journey. How well we plan during this stage will determine how much retracting we will encounter in later stages.

The most ardent achievers will map out what they want to develop both in the long term and also for short term goals. They will lay out a blueprint of their plans. They will work backwards to ascertain what resources will be necessary to reach the goals and what quantity of time it will require.

They use planners and calendars as a few of their favorite preparation tools. They may even in advance fill in dates and information into the calendar weeks, months or even years ahead.

Preparation is not something to take for granted. It will either make you or break you. So prepare well and never cut corners just so save time on this crucial step.

2. Budget Your Time Wisely

A fact of life is that time keeps rushing into the future. People whom are not wise to plan out their goals and schedule to coincide with such aspirations are doomed to not be very productive. Being at your best includes knowing where you want to go in life and take decisive actions to arrive at specific achievement destinations.

Budgeting your time wisely is a skill and a wise habit to practice if you want to get things done. Otherwise, life will pass you by and opportunities to succeed will go to the wayside. Other people who are willing to do the necessary tasks while dedicating themselves to putting in the proper activities plus effort will see fruitful results.

Make daily, weekly and monthly goals. Then keep a planner with you so you can be able to track progress and keep yourself accountable for reaching set goals. Remember to reward yourself at various incremental levels of success so you stay motivated along the way (as I will cover more in Chapter 4 - REWARD YOURSELF FOR VICTORIES).

3. Take a Break to Regain Clarity

All work and no play is a sure path to burn out and boredom. The human mind can only concentrate on any worthwhile subject for short bursts of time. So if we are attempting to force long periods to over-ride our natural circuitry, it will cause undesirable results.

The other issue is that the longer we focus intently on something, the higher the odds are that we lose sight of the bigger scope of what we are developing or learning. Typically, people become so fixated on the small details that they tend to overlook perhaps other points of views that could foment much needed breakthroughs.

We must all take a break every so often to regain clarity of the situation. Even a quick five-minute break to stretch, get some fluids, food in us or go to the bathroom can make a big difference. Then when we return to working on the idea/project, we will be able to problem solve and reach new outcome levels which we never dreamed were possible.

SECTION III
ETHICS

DEFINITION

1) Moral principles that govern a person's behavior or the conducting of an activity.

2) The branch of knowledge that deals with moral principles.

1. Work Hard to Get Results

No one who ever reached the top in any arena ever said it was easy. Only con artists will scam people with the come on lies. These snake oil salesmen types will say that the path to victory is so easy that a 5-year-old can do it. This is definitely not true, in the least. Success does take work, and in some cases a boat load worth. There are no shortcuts for success. You must work hard to get results.

It is true that after you get to a certain point into the process, you have enough foundation and momentum built up where reaching higher elevations of success may be less demanding to reach. Even technology may allow for a certain leverage factors. Still, it took resources such as money or know how to be able to put these tools into action. Even finding the sources to allocate such resources usually takes hard work too.

Keep in mind that in many instances, you may have other people assisting you at that moment, whereby some may actually have been voluntary or paid to assist you. When you originally started out on the path to your goals, you may not have had any help and it may have been only you. So if you have more people working on a project with you, it may not be you specifically that is working hard, yet the entire team effort as a whole is still putting in the hard work.

2. Continually Strive to Do Better

Winners do not accept that they have peaked out and are not capable of improvements. Just because we reach achievement plateaus, it is not a sign that this is the best outcome we could ever get. We must continually strive to do better, regardless how much successes have been bestowed upon us.

The more we know, the more we realize we do not know. Life presents us opportunities for exploring and learning more, if we seek to honor the lessons life presents us through challenges.

Winners will attempt to challenge themselves and see how they can perpetually stretch and grow. They look for ways to improve and refine as time goes on. They are wise enough to comprehend that where attention goes, energy flows and results will show.

Winners grasp that what you ignore or withdraw interaction with, that will experience atrophy. They do not like to have regression, thus will move forward every day with the goal of being a better version of themselves than the day prior.

3. Nobody Likes a Cheater

Some people fear subpar performance, so in order to boost their results, they must artificially find ways to increase the appearance of their task mastery. Even if the person gets away with this sneaky defrauding conduct for the short term or forever, the truth is what matters more.

Some cheaters appear to have no conscious, but a vast majority of them do feel guilt. There will come a point in the future where this cheating activity will start to eat at them so much that the person will completely halt the cheating activities.

Some of the people will come clean that they have been dishonest. Peers may not be so kind, yet time is the ultimate healer for all wounds and indiscretions. Realize that nobody likes a cheater.

Cheaters are able to bluff their way to levels of results that in some cases, only overachievers may accomplish. The risk of being caught as a cheater is never worth the short term reward no matter how great the prize may appear to be.

Keep your integrity and perform the best you can while using your own abilities, no matter how lofty the result becomes. You will sleep super at night knowing you operate from a place of honesty and there will never be an awkward situation to succumb to in the future which could jeopardize all the hard work and years of pursuits you have put in.

4. I Hate Liars

Mom and Dad would always say, "I hate liars!" I agree with them whole heartedly. Liars are the type of people that sabotage good will and hamper on the cooperative spirit of a group of people. Liars are vampires that will suck away the hard work of others in order to claim gains for themselves.

Liars interrupt the harmonizing flow that Winners have propagated. Liars are like septic waste that contaminated clean drinking water; whereby they spew their negativity onto others wherever they go.

Liars are used to making up elaborate stories as they go. They bear false witness to life events and seek to create an unrealistic world that is only favorable to them. In the liar's point of view, they can do no wrong and also must avoid pain at all costs.

They will tell fibs to get out of trouble as well as to divert unwanted attention away from themselves. Liars come across as heartless since they will indiscriminately blame others or put the reputation or safety of others in harm without enough critical forethought.

Hold yourself and others accountable to a high level of moral integrity. Be transparent and keep things genuine. There is no room for "Fake It Till You Make It". "Acting As If" would always be a better solution, since you are not seeking to harm others or yourself with such a life strategy.

Limit your exposure to Liars and surround yourself with others who uphold high standards and prefer to repel turpitude. Make the

ALWAYS DO YOUR BEST

Choice to Not Lie to yourself and others. It is easier to reach great heights of attainment via practicing high integrity.

SECTION IV
MINDSET

DEFINITION

1) The established set of mental attitudes held by someone.

2) An intention or inclination.

3) A person's way of thinking and their opinions

1. Belief Breathes Life into Creating Success

What we regard as true, via magnetic pulling, has the power to create this experience into our reality. Thoughts are living things. They generate uplifting forces that instigate creation to occur. The success masters of our universe will explain to us that we are a byproduct of what we think we are and also what we think about. Hence, belief breathes life into us creating success.

When we choose to not put faith into things, we are sending a signal to our brain that we don't want to attract those very things into our life. Therefore, we will exhibit behaviors, attitudes and thoughts that will repel these things away from us. On the contrary, when we hold strong convictions about wanting to draw affirmative outcomes our way, we are creating pathways inside of our body to get ready to obtain such things.

The lesson here is to believe with all your heart that you will be fortunate in earning the victories you are chasing after. Be a firm believer in the success you desire, regardless of the obstacles at hand. Refrain from holding additional speculations which are contradicting. They are harmful, create instability and overall will get in your way.

Push away the adverse piercing comments of all naysayers. These haters may be jealous of you. Even more dreadful, these party poopers are just bitter over the lack of quality results they received in the past for not being willing to always do their best. Thus, they feel the need to sabotage your victory. Do not listen to them. Run hard to your goals and don't stop believing.

2. Adjust Your Attitude to Propel Your Results

Observe the titans of any field. Do they have an attitude of gratitude or do they have entitlement issues? Do they have an attitude that life sucks and everyone is out to get them or instead do they feel that life is amazing and there are many people they can collaborate with them to reach their intended outcomes?

Do these top producers spend their time feeling sorry for themselves with emotional despair or are they looking to increase their happiness via practical solutions?

Your Attitude will determine your Altitude. Adjust your attitude to propel your results. People who hold on to the pain and live in the regret of what is not working tend to harbor bad attitudes. Shield yourself away from doing so. Protect your attitude at all costs.

Realize that your day is all you got and if you spend the finite time you have in that day feeling down in the dumps, you will bring about meager results. Put your attention on having the best uplifting, flexible attitude you can to maximize your probability for success.

3. Tomorrow is Another Day

Some hustlers believe that there is no tomorrow and the urgency is to get it done today or never. While I love that ambition and intense drive, for many people without an A type personality, it may be a counterproductive way of thinking. For most people out there, they will feel defeated and dejected.

We must not have an all or nothing approach if we want to allow all personality types to embark on success. Grasping a much more flexible policy such as believing Tomorrow is Another Day can lead to an improved coping strategy.

In my opinion, merging the 2 ideologies together correctly can actually preserve the urgency while allowing for us all to win if for some reason we do not finish all of our daily goals today. For instance, we can have a strong conviction that <u>Today Is the Day I Will Do It</u>!

The transition piece will happen at the end of the night when we are accounting for our daily progress results. Only at that final point for that particular day will we changeover to the coping strategy. The strategy would be: <u>I Did Awesome Today and Tomorrow I Will Finish the Goal</u>.

4. REWARD YOURSELF FOR VICTORIES

Imagine a world for a moment where all you did was work, work and then work some more. Now picture yourself receiving no reward in any form for this energy you put in even after some levels of attainment become visible.

How would that make you feel? How long would you continue to work under such dire circumstances? Would you be super human in self-motivation where nothing could stop you, even due to the lack of recognition or brief moments of celebration?

It is crystal clear that the majority of people are not built this way and would not continue onward. As humans, we have a need to feel appreciated and a drive to feel good about what we pursue. Short, small celebrations when we make progress towards a bigger goal is enough to keep us motivated to keep going.

We must reward ourselves for victories. We do not need the validation from others, nor for others to specifically be the ones to give us any reward. If other people do choose to provide these, then so be it.

Something as simple as to treat yourself to your favorite snack when you reach a small milestone will make a big difference to recharging your battery. Medium sized achievements along the way may be rewarded by going out to dinner at a favorite restaurant or buying yourself a modestly priced item you have been wanting.

Reaching big goals are a cause for much celebration, therefore should be met with a larger reward. Such a gift could be a mini trip for you to a destination that has been on your "to do" list. No matter what the rewards end up being, just make sure to practice rewarding yourself for the triumphs you experience as a result of your efforts.

5. You Don't Have to Be First

There are some very good lessons taught in athletics like being a good sport even in the face of defeat. You learn preparation, team work as well as dedication to your craft. There are many other great lessons to be discovered if one is a good student.

However, there is one large and terrible lesson which creates a distortion among people. This is the lesson on competition.

The harmful idea regarding competition is that:

1) There is no value in achieving second place and beyond. Only being number 1 matters and that's all people will remember.

2) Good sportsmanship at the end of a sport event is important to instill community spirit.

In the real life application of this, it does not work this way at all. The way good sportsmanship is utilized, only serves as a saving face grace and is not intended for brotherly/sisterly love towards others, in spite of receiving a game loss. In the locker rooms, the coaches will swear incessantly and yell at the players telling them they are worthless and losers because they did not take 1st place.

Let's make one thing perfectly clear. You don't have to be first place to be a winner. This notion discredits anyone, regardless of effort or obstacles overcome. The competition mindset instills a hostile environment of winner take all and everyone else is irrelevant. Move into more of the mindset that all who show up and work their butt off are important. Praise everyone, yet recognize the ones who are the performers and encourage this behavior. A person is a winner as long as they do their best based on their own abilities.

As long as people are performing, it does not matter what alleged place you end up in. Probability statistics teach us that there are infinitely more people that are working at any given project than the single person who will come in first place for it. Therefore, the wise person sees the flaw in all or nothing philosophy of having to always be number one.

SECTION V
PERFORMANCE

DEFINITION

1) The action or process of carrying out.

2) Accomplishing an action, task, or function.

ALWAYS DO YOUR BEST

1. KEEP YOUR EYES ON YOUR TARGET GOALS

When you drive a vehicle, to get safely to your destination, you better keep your eyes on the road in front of you. Otherwise, there is a strong chance you may have a mishap that will set you back. Similar to driving a vehicle, going after goals works the exact same way.

You must keep your eyes on your target goals. Too much distraction and lack of focal point will lead you to get derailed from reaching your intended goals.

Never allow yourself to forget what your goals are. Written goals are what is important. Goals become concrete and certain for us to go after once we commit to establishing firmly what they precisely are. In this age of technology, even digitally captured goals are fine too.

The next step once you have a written or digital copy of your goal is to keep it fresh in your mind every day. This means that during your morning ritual, you should spend a moment to think about each goal and what you are planning to do that very day to get you closer to reaching it.

In life, there are also many circumstances that get in your way of accomplishing goals. Do not fall prey to being a victim. Dust yourself off, get back up and find your way again to get back on the band wagon of pursuing your goals.

After all, it's not what happens to us, the more distinguished trait is how we handle it. Handle challenges with a can do attitude, since struggles are part of the journey we all face when going after beneficial objectives.

2. Laziness Gets You Nowhere

Apathy is a rapid path to life failure. Laziness is a strong, bad behavior that stems from this sort of careless thinking. Laziness literally gets you nowhere. You will be stuck in a web of be nothing and do nothing, so you can have nothing. Laziness is the twin sister to procrastination.

High achievers are far too busy to just sit around and do nothing. Yet, the people who are trapped in this paradigm, they find themselves to be prisoners to their own indifference of the world around them.

Action is the solution to break this toxic habit. Even the most unproductive activity is still better than none at all. Once a person does finally get started, the next component of activity is to stay consistent.

The third component is for the person to choose the right activities to participate in that will yield the most efficient results. Keep in mind that none of this is an overnight process.

It may take some patience as well as ongoing testing to find what activities work best. Just know that you will experience nirvana just being in do mode and stepping away from the non-productive negative world of apathy.

3. Halfway is No Way

Imagine for a second you are playing a game of basketball. You are a short distance away from the hoop you want to shoot at. However, instead of applying the full amount of energy required to push the basketball from where you stand and score, you only provide half the energy needed.

The question is: Will you get your desired result of getting the ball through the basket and score some points? We both know the obvious answer is no; not by a long shot.

Halfway is no way. No matter what this applied effort is attached to, the consequence is the same. Success can never be yours if you do not give it your best level of effort, focus, energy, and attention. By giving just a small fraction of what is possible, you have effectively robbed yourself of your enormous full potential.

Essentially you would have wasted your time and any resources put in since there will be no visible return on that investment. Instead, always give it 100% of what you got to ensure you will see a return on your efforts.

4. Quitting is Not an Option

It has been said that quitters never win and winners never quit. Quitting is just not a feasible option. How can one be able to hold their head up high and feel proud of their actions if they go around quitting every activity they attempt?

How does a person attain any goals if they give up at the slightest opposition and/or pain felt? What quality would an individual have in their life if they never see a task through to completion to reap the harvest of the efforts they have sewn?

Quitters say things like, "I will TRY this out and see what happens." Winners are well aware that Trying is Lying. What Winner is going to just try something out?

If that were truly the simplest way to obtain victory, companies like Nike would not have chosen the slogan JUST DO IT! Instead, they would have gone with the more proven simple phrase of JUST TRY IT! I'm sure we can all agree that this seems silly and it does not work for securing measurable positive results.

Put your attention on the goals and fall in love with the process. Although the process itself perhaps may not be pleasurable, it is the one thing that will lead you to the happy fruits of your labor. Winners learn to work through the pain and overcome the challenges.

Winners learn to focus on the long game, thus what they are seeking to accomplish. They don't get all hung up on the short game, thereby letting temporary hassles distract them from the big picture of why they are doing the activity to begin with.

5. Excuses are for Losers

Losers love limitations. They love to rationalize away mistakes, defeat, weaknesses, lack of effort, past failures, and any other causes which stopped them from attaining positive outcomes.

Excuses are for losers. They will lie to themselves about why they did not produce quality results and then attempt to sell this same lie to others. The hope is that pity is felt for them and they can have an easy cop-out, thus no need to attempt the task again.

Winners Want Well-Done. They love to jump over, though, around and push past obstacles so that they may ascend to greatness, in spite of any perceived or real challenges. Solutions are for Winners. They will motivate themselves to find ways to produce high quality results and then encourage those around them to do the same.

Winners will even help these other people. Their hope is that inspiration is produced by their outstanding performance, thus they will continue to be high achievers and raise the standards for all around them.

CLOSING

Are you ready to win big in your life? Taking these 20 Life Lessons to heart and apply the principles contained within each. You will be on your way to approach triumph bigger than ever before. Mediocre and disappointing aftermath from your lackluster approaches will be a thing of the past.

Don't just windup reading this book and smirk, reflecting that you just feasted yourself with a pleasurable read. Do something about your situation to favorably influence your life. Create the future that you dream of. Finally, escape from the conflict that holds you a proverbial prisoner. Count on yourself to stimulate the advantageous payoff.

Always Do Your Best. If you ever doubt if what you are doing is your best, just re-read this book again and rehash the 20 Life Lessons once more. I can promise you that by utilizing these concepts into your life, you will be able to Always Do Your Best and tangibly reap amazing rewards. I believe in you and know you can do this. Now go out there and make your life happen.

Thank You!

Marc Shamus

About the Author

Marc Shamus is a teacher of life strategies and ideas that may improve the quality of the people's lives. He is a Published Author, Life Educator, Public Speaker and Entrepreneur.

Learn more about Marc at:
iMasterLife.com/MarcShamus

Learn more about Marc's Publishing Company at:
iMasterLife.com

Personal Dedication

This book is very personal to me. I want to give the deepest appreciation to my father, Richard Shamus and mother, Phyllis Shamus, who pushed me my whole life to excel and did not accept anything but my best at all times. "I LOVE YOU!".

April 27, 2003 Dad and Mom

DID YOU LOVE <u>ALWAYS DO YOUR BEST</u>?

Thank you for investing in yourself and in this book.

If you enjoyed this book, please let others know how much they can benefit from it by leaving a review here:

iMasterLife.com/Reviews/Shamus3

If you have feedback on how to make this book even better, I'd love to hear it at **info@imasterlife.com**

Thanks!

Marc Shamus

Thanks again for your support!

MORE RECOMMENDED PUBLICATIONS

Go to:

iMasterLife.com/develop

WATCH OUR VIDEO COURSES

Get access to training video courses by going to
iMasterLife.com/Courses

Inside these course, you'll discover...

• What are the <u>Basics</u> of each taught subject

• How to <u>Make</u> <u>Your</u> <u>Life</u> <u>Better</u> as you learn & apply lessons

• How <u>Powerful</u> "YOU" really are

www.ingramcontent.com/pod-product-compliance
Lightning Source LLC
Chambersburg PA
CBHW071647040426
42452CB00009B/1794